I'M A BUZZ BUZZ BEE.

LEARN ABOUT ME!

Written and Illustrated by Gosia Kozdron
First Published in the United Kingdom, 2021

DID YOU KNOW that bees are some of the most important creatures that help our planet grow? Our buzzing friends are responsible for one out of every three bites of food we eat, and it's oh so sweet!

Buzzing bees were alive and stinging
even when the dinos were singing.

There are more than 20,000 species of bees. They live on every continent except Antarctica because they would freeze!

Bees live in hives and are divided into three kinds their whole lives.

QUEEN, DRONES, AND WORKERS

Drones, the male bees have bigger eyes to help them find the Queen Bee in the skies.

Worker bees collect pollen and nectar to feed the community. They clean the hive, make the honey and take care of the queen in unity.

Bees build their hives in places that are hard to get to, so animals don't disturb their working crew.

They protect themselves by stinging with ease.

But bees that are out, away from their hive, usually won't sting to survive. They are keen on finding pollen and returning to their Queen. They aren't mean!

Bees eat nectar and pollen from flowers. Nectar is very sugary and gives them energy for hours!

The colour and flavour of honey depend on where the bees buzz and collect their nectar with no fuss!

There are 300 uNiQUE types of honey, each originating from a different flower, how funny!?

If you want more busy bees in your garden, then grow more flowers. They love bright colours! The blue, purple, and yellow are their favourite, and they give them powers!

Bees are very hardworking and seem to have endless energy. It takes a bee their whole lifetime to produce the best teaspoon of honey there will ever be.

So to make a jar of honey, we need 200 bees working super hard in your backyard.

The bee is the only insect that can be tamed. People built hives to secure them a safe and healthy home. They are placed in gardens where busy bees can roam.

Worker Bees use waggle dancing to communicate. When they find flowers, that's how they tell their mate.

Bees are known to steal honey by sneaking into other hives.
But, if they get caught, they get into a battle for their lives!

Our buzzing friends can beat their wings 200 times per second!
It lets them fly fast from one flower to another.

Now you know more about buzz, buzz bees,
so you can feel at ease!

Printed in Great Britain
by Amazon

15969818R00016